In Her Feminine Sign

Dunya Mikhail

—

In Her Feminine Sign

A New Directions Paperbook Original

Manufactured in the United States of America
New Directions Books are printed on acid-free paper
First published as a New Directions Paperbook (NDP1454) in 2019
Book design and typesetting by Eileen Baumgartner

Library of Congress Cataloging-in-Publication Data
Names: Mikhail, Dunya, 1965– author.
Title: In her feminine sign / Dunya Mikhail.
Other titles: Poems. Selections. English
Description: New York : New Directions, 2019. | "A New Directions paperbook original." | Includes bibliographical references.
Identifiers: LCCN 2019011201 | ISBN 9780811228763 (alk. paper)
Classification: LCC PJ7846.I392 A2 2019 | DDC 892.7/16—dc23
LC record available at https://lccn.loc.gov/2019011201

10 9 8 7 6 5 4 3 2 1

New Directions Books are published for James Laughlin
by New Directions Publishing Corporation
80 Eighth Avenue, New York 10011
ndbooks.com

Contents

T/here

Author's Note

I wrote these poems from right to left and from left to right, in Arabic and in English. I didn't translate them; I only wrote them twice. Writing these poems in two languages maybe makes a new "original." This process somehow liberated me from having to follow the first text, particularly when the second text came first, given the cultural connotation. To capture the poem in two lives is to mirror my exile, with all of its possibilities and risks. But as home is flashed through exile, a poem is sometimes born on the tip of another tongue.

It was annoying to me in the beginning when my poem pulled me right and left, but I always follow my poetry, just as people say to "follow your heart." Well, to justify my choice, I would claim that allowing such a dialogue between the two texts is democratic, and even hopeful that East and West may meet in that crossing line between two languages. But this is not to say that I've achieved a linguistic utopia. To produce a text in two languages is to always hold a mirror to the first text while the mirror behaves as if that text is actually her mirror. The poet is at home in both texts, yet she remains a stranger. This English edition shows readers one side of the mirror.

The Tied Circle

The Stranger in Her Feminine Sign

Everything has gender
in Arabic:
History is male.
Fiction is female.
Dream is male.
Wish is female.

Feminine words are followed
by a circle with two dots over it.
They call this symbol "the tied circle,"
knotted with wishes
which come true only when forgotten
or replaced by the wishes of others.

In the town of tied wishes
people feel great anticipation
because a stranger will arrive
today in her feminine sign.
Someone says he saw her
two dots glittering,
refuting another's vision
of a cat's eyes hunting in darkness.
So scary, he says, *how the moon
hides in her red circle.*

Everyone is busy today
listing wishes on pieces
of paper they'll give to the wind.
When the stranger finds them
on her way, she'll collect them
and adorn them to her circle,

tossing off some old wishes
to make space for the new.
They say the dropped ones
will come true.

The stranger's lateness
worries those who wait.
Someone says she's searching
for a word to complete
a special sentence,
the gift she'll bring to town.

Another wonders if she seeks
a verb or a noun,
and offers to find her.
A third warns that the stranger
may turn him, with one touch,
into a flower that blooms
for only an instant
before it withers and dies,
her circle throbbing with songs
that cause sadness and elation
and something so obscure
no one has a name for it.
Will she complete a verb
or a noun phrase—or go solo,
a word complete on its own?
They wonder.

When they finally hear footsteps,
they know the stranger must be near.
Make sure the gate is open,
they remind one another.
They hear clinking—
A bracelet? A chain?

Song Inside a Fossil

She's still looking
down at her baby
after 4,800 years.
Her fossil has the curve
of mothers telling
endless stories in the dark.
There were three birds
in the cage, she says.
Two died of poisoned water.
Though birds don't know
what poison means,
the survivor has the memory
of thirst and of two silent birds.

If birds' memories are circles, a line
must bisect them, tracing their migration
to places that are neither homelands nor exiles.

But what if the world, for birds,
is all exile, till they leave it behind?

The day her baby came into the world,
she carried water to him in her voice.
She sung so close, he could hear
her heart beat like a bass drum.

He won't remember the seeds
her words scatter, but won't forget
the debris of what was shattered
from every wingbeat recalling her.

Birds don't know
what coming to this world means,
but the bird who survived sings.

Is it an elegy for the two silent birds,
or a way of coming back to life?

Their circular embrace is
a song inside a fossil,
life in a cage.

Baghdad in Detroit

On the Fourth of July
here in Detroit
I hear the echo of Baghdad explosions.
They say it is the sound of fireworks.

Song by song
I scatter my birds
away from the fog of smoke.
They say it is ordinary clouds in the sky.

A butterfly from the Tigris shore
alights on my hand.
No bombs today to scare her away.
They say this is the Detroit River.

I enter a shelter
with the others in the crowd.
We will leave at the end of the raid.
They say this is the tunnel to Canada.

Plastic Death

In my childhood
in Baghdad
we played dead:
we killed each other
with plastic weapons.
We lay on the floor,
still as corpses
for a minute
or two.
Then one of us laughed,
exposing our plastic death;
we held each other
as the dying might
life itself, but rose
to play another game.
The years turn over
and Baghdad recedes
with our childhoods
into exile.
From afar, we see children
who look like we did.
They kill each other,
lie motionless
on the floor.
But none of them laugh
or hold life
and rise.

Nisaba

How shall I call you
when you have one hundred names?

I say *Nisaba*
and I mean praises for the little things,
I mean the big things, or rather
the little things with their big shadows:

the number to round off
the killed ones to zero

the chalk held by a girl
who draws for the world
a circle with everyone inside

the open wings
over the fires

the soft moss
briefly visible
through the river
like the faces of the absentees

the comma between
death and life

the everyday practice
of the doctor
with the stethoscope
pressed against a chest

the blue flower
in Novalis's dream.

Salwa

She has no map,
only songs for places
she will cross and forget.

She hums in secret
and when words don't come
she borrows the rhythm of the road,
fast and slow.
The birds understand.
They answer in secret, too.

She doesn't care much
about transformations
between day and night
although she's puzzled
and amazed by the moon,
how it passes her by
like a train disappearing
with its passengers
until it stops at the last station,
alone at last.

She waits for no one.
History is dried blood
in her lipstick.
She applies it now
to kill the moment
or beautify it a little.

She knows the time
from the way the roses bend,
from the farness or nearness of the sky,
from the dryness in her hands.

When she tires
of wandering,
she sits in the shade
and with her little stick,
she draws on the earth's floor
the face of someone
she doesn't know.

Eva Whose Shadow Is a Swan

The day we met in Babylon
for me to interpret her,
Eva found a pocket stone
she'd later add to her collection
of stones from different cities
she kept in a glass bowl.

We strolled roadsides
piled with rocks blasted
from bridges and buildings
now bent and cratered,
yet I like to think that stone
might have predated the fall of Babylon,
when people spoke one language.

I liked Eva's musical tone.
She said, *I am from Stockholm,*
home to no war for two hundred years.

I am from Baghdad, I replied,
a city we call the "home of peace,"
though war has lived in it
for two hundred years.

We exchanged postcards
for thirty years before my East
and her West met in London,
our friendship needing
no umbrellas in the rain.
I waited for her impatiently
but hid on a whim behind a pillar,

admiring her poise
as she approached
and scanned the passersby,
like Noah in search of the Ark.

A woman nearly ninety,
so beautiful,
her shadow a swan,
a goddess who found
her lost universe in the last minute.

She hiked an island mountain
on the way to our meeting
and bought a CD
of ferry music for me.

When I followed up
with a farewell call, I learned
she'd lost her hearing:
Write, so I can hear you.

She must have read my lips—
the concert we attended
in the rain must have seemed
like lightning without thunder.

When I receive her postcard,
I can't read her handwriting
but plan to search the dictionary
of Babylon for her words
and decipher the line drawn by time.

Three Women

Another night on the way to the cages
and the stars—dead eggs glistening—
don't know the secret of the stone.

For ten years the stone was left
in the basement with the three
kidnapped women inside it.

Their souls broke the door and escaped.
Their bodies lagged a few steps behind.
They will never look back.

If they do, they will find their feathers
scattered everywhere, and a bell
with no ring, and three shadows

trapped inside a stone.

My Grandmother's Grave

When my grandmother died
I thought, *She can't die again.*
Everything in her life
happened once and forever:
her bed on our roof,
the battle of good and evil in her tales,
her black clothes,
her mourning for her daughter
killed by headaches,
the rosary beads and her murmur,
Forgive us our sins,
her empty vase from the Ottoman time,
her braid, each hair a history.
The Sumerians were first,
their dreams inscribed in clay tablets.
They drew palms, the dates
ripening before their sorrows.
They drew an eye to chase evil
away from their city.
They drew circles and prayed for them:
a drop of water
a sun
a moon
a wheel spinning faster than Earth.
They begged, *O gods, don't die and leave us alone.*

Over the tower of Babel,
light is exile, blurred,
its codes crumbs of songs
leftover for the birds.

More naked emperors
passed by the Tigris
and more ships...
the river full
of crowns
helmets
books
dead fish,
and on the Euphrates
corpse-lilies float.

Every minute a new hole formed
in the body of the ship.

The clouds descended on us
war by war,
picked up our years,
our hanging gardens,
and flew away like storks.

We said nothing worse could come.
Then the barbarians arrived
at the mother of two springs.
They broke my grandmother's grave—my clay tablet.
They smashed the winged bulls whose eyes
were wide open
sunflowers
watching the fragments of our first dreams
for a lifetime.
My hand brushes the map
as if rubbing an old scar.

100 Years of Sleep

I don't want to be the princess.
I only want to be her sleep
for 100 years.

I want to skip the problems
of the twenty-first century—
water pollution
nuclear war
capsized boats
that carry immigrants
away from their homelands.

I may miss important inventions
and new songs
and weekends
when people go out
on their dates
followed by one moon.

I may open my eyes for a moment
to take a glimpse of the universe in its beauty
and then close them again.

But what if my loved ones
surrounded me
and whispered in my ear
one by one?
I would wake up of course.

My Poem Will Not Save You

Remember the toddler lying face down
on the sand, and the waves gently receding
from his body as if a forgotten dream?

My poem will not turn him onto his back
and lift him up
to his feet
so he can run
into a familiar lap
like before.
I am sorry
my poem will not
block the shells
when they fall
onto a sleeping town,
will not stop the buildings
from collapsing
around their residents,
will not pick up the broken-leg flower
from under the shrapnel,
will not raise the dead.
My poem will not defuse
the bomb
in the public square.
It will soon explode
where the girl insists
that her father buy her gum.
My poem will not rush them
to leave the place
and ride the car
that will just miss the explosion.

Many mistakes in life
will not be corrected by my poem.
Questions will not be answered.
I am sorry
my poem will not save you.
My poem cannot return
all of your losses,
not even some of them,
and those who went far away
my poem won't know how to bring them back
to their lovers.
I am sorry.
I don't know why the birds
sing
during their crossings
over our ruins.
Their songs will not save us,
although, in the chilliest times,
they keep us warm,
and when we need to touch the soul
to know it's not dead,
their songs
give us that touch.

Tablets

II

1

I close my eyes and see a dot.
It becomes a spot of light.
It grows into the size of a person
who moves into the distance
until it returns to a spot of light,
a dot.

2

Like communion bread
your words dissolve in my mouth
and never die.

3

I don't care under which sky—
just sing your song till the end.

4

The bone-city I am choked by
is also salt
also sugar
also boiling water
in the kettle without a lid.

5

Ask not how many houses were built.
Ask how many residents remained in the houses.

6

The flame opens like a giant plant
swallowing them one by one
with their lost-and-found sheep.

7

She whose song
has no beginning
or end;
she whose voice
faded into stars and moons...
Where is she?
Where is she?

8

There are two types of dreams:
vertical and horizontal.
Tell me the shape of your dream
and I will tell you where you are from.

9

Fire and light
both sting.
We go to sleep when the other half
of the globe wakes up.
Night and day
crowded with dreams.

10

Your look
passes through me
like lightning.

11

The butterfly that flew a moment ago
over the killed ones
was a soul
searching for home.

12

Our time together
has ripened, now
smashed like berries.

13

Can your camera capture
fear in the eyes
of the mother sparrow, see
the broken eggs in her eyes?

14

A little air means so much for the bird.
In the air, a full world extends.
The clouds gather and then separate.
The leaves wave to each other.
For the bird, everything hangs in the air.

15

The pomegranate seeds
scattered with our steps
were not from heaven.

16

My paper boat that drifted into the river
with the world behind it
had a special note.
It may arrive one day,
albeit late,
all truths come late.

17

Dried leaves
over there:
our first yearnings.

18

The shoes by the door
will not fit them when they return.

19

She counts the pebbles by her fingers.
The other pebbles underwater
are losses outside her hands.

20

Specks of sand
fell down
from the fingers:
our people.

21

The sun reveals
a hole in the boat,
a glow in the fins
of fish still breathing.

22
The day and the night
divide our steps on the road
as they equally
divide the world.

23
I was born.
I write poetry.
I will die.

24
Her shadow
is still here
feeding the birds.

III

1

Like the turtle,
I walk everywhere
with my home on my back.

2

The mirror on the wall
doesn't show any of the faces
that used to pass
in front of it.

3

The dead
act like the moon:
they leave the Earth behind
and move away.

4

Oh, little ants,
how you move forward
without looking back.
If I could only borrow your steps.

5

All of us are autumn leaves
ready to fall at any time.

6

The spider makes a home outside itself.
It doesn't call it exile.

7
Forgotten
faces of the dead
as if we had only met once
through revolving doors.

8
I am not a pigeon
knowing my way home.

9
Just like that
they packed our green years
to feed a hungry sheep.

10
Of course you can't see the word love.
I wrote it on water.

11
When the moon is full
it looks like a zero.
Life is round
at the end.

12
The grandfather left the country with one suitcase.
The father left with empty hands.
The son left with no hands.

13
No, I am not bored of you.
The moon, too, appears every day.

14
She drew her pain:
a colorful stone
settled deep inside the sea.
The fish pass by
and can't touch it.

15
She was safe
inside her mother's belly.

16
The lanterns know the value of night,
and are more patient
than the stars.
They stay until morning.

17
Those colorful flowers
over the mass graves
are the dead's last words.

18
The Earth is so simple—
you can explain it with a tear or a laugh.
The Earth is so complicated—
you need a tear or a laugh
to explain it.

19
The number you see now
will inevitably change
with the next dice roll.
Life won't show its faces
all at once.

20
I love you
in the singular
even though I use the plural,
both the regular and irregular plurals.

21
The sweet moment is over.
I spent an hour
thinking of that moment.

22
The butterfly brings pollen
with its little feet, and flies away.
The flower can't follow it—
its leaves flutter,
and its crown grows wet
with tears.

23
Some of our tribal members
died in war, some
died regular deaths.
None of them died from joy.

24
That woman standing in the public square
is made of bronze.
She's not for sale.

IV

1

I wanted to write an epic about suffering,
but when I found a tendril
of her hair among the ruins
of her mud house
I found my epic there.

2

I didn't sleep last night.
It was as if the night
itself hid in the morning coffee.

3

Her life is a game of snakes and ladders
sent relentlessly back to square one,
but whose life isn't like this? She takes
a breath and throws the dice again.

4

The city glitters below
the airplane window, not because
of the bones and skulls scattered
under the sun, but the view
through the frosted porthole.

5

She died, and time changed
for those she loved most,
but her watch kept ticking.

6

A god carried the burdens
until the weight persuaded him
to transfer them to man:
the new suffering god.

7

The map of Iraq looks like a mitten
and so does the map of Michigan—
a match I made by chance.

8

If you can't save people
at least don't hate them.

9

Her bubbling annoys me—
I can't understand a word she says.
So what if I toss her from the aquarium?
So what if I spill her new world
with this nasty immigrant fish?

10

The city's innumerable lights
turning on and off remind us
we are born to arrive
as we are born to leave.

11

The handkerchiefs are theirs,
but the tears are ours.

12

Women running barefoot.
Behind them, stars falling from the sky.

13

So strange
that in my dream of us
you were also a dream.

14

He said to me: *You are in my eyes.*
Now when he sleeps,
his eyelids cover me.

15

Gilgamesh stopped wishing
for immortality,
for only in death could he be certain
of seeing his friend Enkidu again.

16

Some say love means
putting all your eggs
in one basket.
If they all break,
can the basket remain intact?

17

The homeless are not afraid
to miss something.
The world passes before their eyes
as clouds pass over rushing cars
pigeons miss some of the seeds
on the road and step away.
Yet only the homeless know
what it means to have a home
and to return to it.

18

The wind and rain
batter us
without discrimination.
We are equal
in the eyes of the storm.

19

When I was broken into fragments
you puzzled me
back together
piece by piece.
I no longer fear
being broken
at any moment.

20

Freezing in the mountains
without blankets or food,
and all they heard was
no news is good news.

21

Their stories didn't kill me
but l would die if l didn't
tell them to you.

22

Before killing them
they collected their personal effects.
Their cell phones are all ringing
in the box.

23

We are not upset when
the grass dies. We know
it will come back
in a season or two.
The dead don't come back
but they appear every time
in the greenness of the grass.

24

If yearning encircles us,
what does it mean?
That a circle has no beginning
and no end?

V

1

Light falls from her voice
and I try to catch it as the last
light of the day fades...
But there is no form to touch,
no pain to trace.

2

Are dreams
taking their seats
on the night train?

3

She recites a list of wishes
to keep him from dying.

4

The truth lands like a kiss—
sometimes like a mosquito,
sometimes like a lantern.

5

Your coffee-colored skin
awakens me to the world.

6

We have only one minute
and I love you.

7

All children are poets
until they quit the habit
of reaching for butterflies
that are not there.

8

The moment you thought you lost me,
you saw me clearly
with all of my flowers,
even the dried ones.

9

If you pronounce all letters
and vowels at once,
you would hear their names
falling drop by drop
with the rain.

10

We carved
our ancestral trees into boats.
The boats sailed into harbors
that looked safe from afar.

11

Trees talk to each other
like old friends
and don't like to be interrupted.
They follow anyone who
cuts one of them,
turning that person
into a lonely cut branch.
Is this why in Arabic
we say "cut of a tree"
when we mean
"having no one"?

12

The way roots hide
under trees—
there are secrets,
faces, and wind
behind the colors
in Rothko's untitled canvases.

13

Will the sea forget its waves,
as caves forgot us?

14

Back when there was no language
they walked until sunset
carrying red leaves
like words to remember.

15

It's true that pain
is like air, available
everywhere,
but we each feel
our pain hurts the most.

16

So many of them died
under stars
that don't know their names.

17

If she just survived with me.

18

A flame dims in the fireplace,
a day slips quietly away from the calendar,
and Fairuz sings, "They say love kills time,
and they also say time kills love."

19

The street vendor offers tourists
necklaces with divided hearts,
seashells to murmur the sea's secrets in your ear,
squishy balls to make you feel better,
maps of homelands you fold
in your pocket as you go on your way.

20

I am haunted by the melody
of a forgotten song
sung while two hands
tied my shoelaces into a ribbon
and waved me goodbye to school.

21

If I could photocopy
the moment we met
I would find it full
of all the days and nights.

22

It won't forget the faraway child,
that city whose door stayed open
for passersby, tourists, and invaders.

23

The moon is going to the other
side of the world
to call my loved ones.

24

The seasons change
colors and you come and go.
What color is your departure?

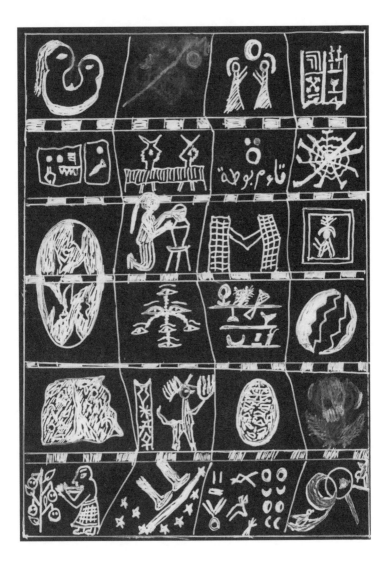

T/here

What We Carry to Mars

This new tablet you carry contains text and images of what's remembered from Earth. You saved your life in the cloud, and now you are traveling with it to Mars.

You can't open a window on the way, to take a look at Mother Earth, not even a last look. Like any other mother, she will not stop spinning around the sun, though her residents never really feel her movement.

Mothers are circles with cracks. As Leonard Cohen said, "There is a crack in everything, that's how the light gets in."

Save that in the "Words as Vitamins for the Soul" file.

It doesn't matter if you forget something; you may simply go to the cloud and download your memories. Sometimes you smile. I know, sometimes you want to forget.

We are all refugees. We move on, feeling that we've left something behind.

You don't exactly know what you miss.

"Faraway" is a relative word. The theory of place we've been discussing for a lifetime will have another meaning over there.

Time will not be the same either. "I see you in a year of light" means "See you later."

The hour will have no minutes. There will be just dust in a tube, and we can flip the tube over to see when we can return, just like this.

How many departures can you put up with?

"Are we safe there?" you wonder.
Are we safe here? Forget safety.

Here you have plants and no time to water them.

There you have time and no plants to water.

Here Earth has gravity so you don't fly, and at the end you return to Mother Earth.

The Sumerians said "returning to the mother" when they meant "freedom." See my poem "Ama-ar-gi" for further possibilities.

On Mars, where do they bury the dead?

There is less gravity there and thus enough to fly.

When you fly, cages become the last expectation.

T/here simple warmth, which is the difference between "living" and "alive."

Mars looks like a half-baked cake.

No god yet to punish the sinners or console the sad ones.

The new planet is almost empty, but the word "empty" is relative too. The sky looks "empty" but it's stuffed with stories we invented for the angels and devils. Our grandmothers, too, used to stuff our pillows with feathers and stories they had invented for us.

You are not sure where you should start from. So much war and so much love. You pack it all up and parachute to the new place like any immigrant with dreams and chimeras and dying stars.

A free dandelion, you are carried away in the wind, while in the background you hear "Songs from the Time of Earth" from someone's tablet. Is it nostalgia or accident? You are not sure.

Ama-ar-gi

Scattered, like us, the Sumerian letters.

"Freedom" is inscribed
Ama-ar-gi, meaning
"returning to the mother."

This, then, is how the map grew borders.
The birds don't know it yet, leaving
their droppings wherever they want.
Their songs, like exiles, might pass by

anywhere. There are no borders
in paradise, neither spoils nor victors.
Paradise is Ama-ar-gi,
no victors at all.

There are no borders in hell,
no losses no demons.
Hell is Ama-ar-gi,
no demons at all.

Ama-ar-gi might be a moon
that follows us home, a shadow
that stumbles on its true self,
a bead from a bracelet,
a secret a tree keeps for centuries.
Maybe it's what crowds the prisoner's heart,
or what shines around the pebbles
mixed with drops of water

among the rocks, what seeps out
from the dead into our dreams.
Maybe it's a flower thrown into the air
and hangs there alone,
a flower that will live and die without us.

Ama-ar-gi—
that's how we return to the mother,
strangers from strangers.

And so like all of you,
we breathe Ama-ar-gi
and before we shed our first tears
Ama-ar-gi is what we weep.

That Place

I want that place
and you in it as always:
how you remember my flower
kept in the refrigerator.

I want that place
and I in it as always:
the candy moon we put
under our pillows
to dream of those who will love
us tomorrow.

I know the trees
in your garden and how they grow
quietly like grandmothers,
and how the gravity pulls light
into your hands.

Black and White

In chess,
white plays first
and black responds.
When a challenge happens,
killing offers the easiest solution.

The two players alternate
tossing wooden bodies into the box.
The pawns are the first to go.

A tie ends it:
everybody died,
except the black king and the white king,
separated by a borderline
and a memory of ruined castles.

The two kings are afraid
of losing one another.
The problem is how to meet

without a checkmate.
Love offers the hardest solution.
The rules of the game dictate
that sharing a square
equals death for one

and keeping their distance
means death for them both.
To leave the board

for a life the color
of water, a play
no less risky
than running after a bubble:
you lose it once you touch it.

The War in Colors

The digital map on the wall
displays American wars
in colors:
Iraq in purple
Syria in yellow
Kuwait in blue
Afghanistan in red
Vietnam in green.
The war
on the map
is beautiful.

N ن

The "N" on the doors,
an exodus
from houses:
no keys
no compass
no words.

Wide clothes
cover tightened souls.
Lights tremble
in the lanterns.

How heavy the carriage is!
It carries the skies
on their shoulders,
along with their sorrows,
the phantoms of those
taken aside,
and the last looks.
It carries the newborn
startled from the shake
of the wheels.
It carries a schoolbag
with the colorful wars
in a history book,
the atlas made of what is
remembered,
the math book and its questions
multiplying like the weight
of the carriage.

The moon doesn't reflect
what is carried
or left behind.
Like them, it's waning.

The "N" on the doors
is a rainbow
drained of color
and the dot above
it is a lonely god.

Tomorrow the Earth will turn
with their fields,
with early fallen leaves
as if shaken off by the trees.
The Earth will turn
with their shops full of timepieces,
antiques, and suitcases;
the dust will fall off
their ancient stuff,
but something they can't fix
will land on their chests
like a sunset.

Tomorrow they will gather
what remains:
mud stuck on their shoes,
kite sticks,
safety pins, and buttons,
a distant star in the dark.
Tomorrow they will
make a country
from the straw
and from whatever else remains.

The "N"
is a lap
in the mountain.
Every grain a bell
relentlessly ringing.

Where will the ringing carry them?
How many will survive
to return someday
and see the pictures
of the dead on the walls?

How many girls will outgrow
their dresses
while on the road?
Countries grow smaller
behind the backs
of the departing ones.

The "N"
and the pen
and the footsteps
and the late sun
and their crumpled shadows
on the walls of the cave.

Sisyphus, exhausted,
left his rock for us,
and when my turn came
I paused
to ask about my father.
Did he emerge from the whale?
Did he leave his bed when he was sick?
Did he die from thirst?

The rock opened its mouth:
I didn't see your father
for twenty years ... and who are you?

I am the child who ran
to seek the ones who hid—
she screamed for them to come out
or else she would quit the game.

I am the stranger who forgot
to put out the fire
and now, having returned
to collect the scattered feathers
in the ash, suddenly sees
her own wrinkles in the map.

I am the village on the hillside.
They left my doors open
and left. They didn't
tie their shoelaces.
No doughs rise in the ovens
this evening.

No
one
is here
under
the sun.

Nuun
Nuuna
Nye

Nye for little Mariam.
She made sandals
from tree leaves
to wear
in the caravan.

Nye for Khudayda.
He didn't bury his family.
Frozen and tearful—a half-melted glacier
and their photos in his hands.

Nye for the child.
They don't know his name
or where his parents are.
His quiet gaze, a flash
of lightning in the eyelids.

Nye for the mother.
Which child to save first?
She sang
the same lullaby
to each of them.

Nye for our people.
They fell before
their fruits could fall,
and the grass grows
around their sleep
without memory
as it grows
elsewhere.

On the Edge of a Mass Grave

He sleeps on his side,
as usual, except his bones
are visible—
you can even count them.

Surrounded by friends,
as usual, except they're dead.
He's completely calm
and doesn't worry about his wounds.

The sun slips through the clouds
above the mass grave
as usual, except today
it brightens death.

They are close to each other
like conjoined trees
on which they would rest their backs
except now they have no words.

Bare hands
↓
search
↓
for someone
↓
maybe alive
↓
but stuck in the void
↓
between the debris
↓
suddenly skyless
↓
a bird
↓
stuffed with dust
↓
a rake
↓
digs for something
↓
missing
↓
→   →   **On Ground Zero**   →   →

in flight
↑
vaporized
↑
as butterflies
↑
under scorched leaves
↑
lay hidden
↑
as if eternity
↑
no traces remain
↑
with flashing lights
↑
once crossed streets
↑
footsteps
↑
and strange
↑
now still
↑

The Others

We are not dead,
and those are not our ghosts.
We don't know where they came from,
or where they are going.
Their shadows are as changeable
as the moon's phases
and are not our shapes.
Their jinns floating over the waters
are not our wars.
Their hollows are not our cracks
on the walls. In our sleep,
they melt into one gesture.
What do they want to say?
And why—every night,
in view of the stars—do they dig
a hole for someone whose turn has come?
They call on us,
and we are in the middle of the river.
They carry their perforated jars.
We count the holes,
and they count our memories.

To catch their fears
we set fires. To imitate us
they light up our darkness.
We will abandon them, we say,
and they will slip away like a passing idea,
beam of light
that doesn't know where to fall.

We pretend it's not dry yet,
the life we left
on the string,
and go and look for their voices.
Like them we hide.
Between one dream and another,
we hear their wooden steps.
We call on them
and they are in the middle
of the river.

Drawing

She called him "River"
and herself "Fish."
One day she sent him
a drawing of a fish on land
and a river with an "X" across it.
He shriveled up quickly
at this separation, worrying
if she meant
he was dead to her, or if
she meant she was dead
without him.

Flamingo

I read that flamingoes
have migrated back to Iraq

after a twenty-year absence,
and I bend my head,

imitating the perfect,
half-hearted Valentine

shape they make in pairs.
I wait for you

at the lake's edge
standing on one leg.

The moon I swallow
when I open my beak

and fly home to you
will be full.

Rotation

I don't feel the rotation of the Earth,
not even when I see
the cities moving backward
through the train's window,
one by one.

Not even when I return
each time to the same place
where birds pick up the mornings
with their beaks and spread them away
as new circles of light.

Not even when I sleep
and see you alive in my dream
and then wake knowing the dead
didn't rise yet from their death.

Not even when I find myself
saying the same thing over and over
as if those words were oars
cutting through a river
we cross in turns
with our untold stories
to that same shore, in silence.

Notes

p. 11   *The Stranger in Her Feminine Sign*: In Arabic, there's a feminine symbol (a circle with two dots above it that appears at the end of the word) used to transform a masculine word into a feminine one.

p. 13   *Song Inside a Fossil*: In 2016, archaeologists in Taiwan uncovered the ancient remains of a young mother cradling an infant child in a 4,800-year-old embrace.

p. 17   *Nisaba*: The Sumerian goddess of writing.

p. 23   *Three Women*: This poem was written in 2013, after the story broke about a man who had imprisoned three women in his basement in Cleveland, Ohio for nearly a decade, using them as sex slaves.

p. 29   *Tablets*: The first section of "Tablets"—my attempt to write Iraqi haiku—can be found in *The Iraqi Nights*. The Sumerian clay tablets come down to us as the earliest recorded communication in history. I tried to imitate those ancient symbols with the drawings that accompany the poems.

p. 64   *N ن*: *Nuun* is the name of the letter "N," which has been marked on the doors of minority groups by Daesh in cities in northern Iraq as a warning to leave home or get killed. *Nuuna*: "whale" in Aramaic. *Nye*: "flute" in Arabic; an instrument usually heard in sad songs in Iraq.

Acknowledgments

Thanks to the editors of the following publications in which some of these poems first appeared: *Amberflora*; *Ambit*; *Consequence*; *Cortland Review*; *Fifth Wednesday Journal*; *Grub Street*; ∞ *Mile*; *International Journal of Contemporary Iraqi Studies*; *The Missing Slate*; *Pea River Journal*; *Poetry*; *Modern Poetry in Translation*; *Quarter After Eight*; *Spacecraft; Transmission*; *War, Literature & the Arts*; and *World Literature Today*.

And my heartfelt thanks to the following poets for their exceptional support: Joy Harjo, Edward Hirsch, Jane Hirshfield, Naomi Shihab Nye, Maggie Smith, Brian Turner, Jeffrey Yang, and Adam Zagajewski. I believe that two groups of people benefit the most from encouragement: children and poets.

New Directions Paperbooks — a partial listing

Federico García Lorca, Selected Poems*
   Three Tragedies
Nathaniel Mackey, Splay Anthem
Xavier de Maistre, Voyage Around My Room
Stéphane Mallarmé, Selected Poetry and Prose*
Javier Marías, Your Face Tomorrow (3 volumes)
Harry Mathews, The Solitary Twin
Bernadette Mayer, Works & Days
Carson McCullers, The Member of the Wedding
Thomas Merton, New Seeds of Contemplation
   The Way of Chuang Tzu
Henri Michaux, A Barbarian in Asia
Dunya Mikhail, The Beekeeper
Henry Miller, The Colossus of Maroussi
   Big Sur & the Oranges of Hieronymus Bosch
Yukio Mishima, Confessions of a Mask
   Death in Midsummer
   Star
Eugenio Montale, Selected Poems*
Vladimir Nabokov, Laughter in the Dark
   Nikolai Gogol
   The Real Life of Sebastian Knight
Raduan Nassar, A Cup of Rage
Pablo Neruda, The Captain's Verses*
   Love Poems*
Charles Olson, Selected Writings
George Oppen, New Collected Poems
Wilfred Owen, Collected Poems
Michael Palmer, The Laughter of the Sphinx
Nicanor Parra, Antipoems*
Boris Pasternak, Safe Conduct
Kenneth Patchen
   Memoirs of a Shy Pornographer
Octavio Paz, Poems of Octavio Paz
Victor Pelevin, Omon Ra
Alejandra Pizarnik
   Extracting the Stone of Madness
Ezra Pound, The Cantos
   New Selected Poems and Translations
Raymond Queneau, Exercises in Style
Qian Zhongshu, Fortress Besieged
Raja Rao, Kanthapura
Herbert Read, The Green Child
Kenneth Rexroth, Selected Poems
Keith Ridgway, Hawthorn & Child
Rainer Maria Rilke
   Poems from the Book of Hours
Arthur Rimbaud, Illuminations*
   A Season in Hell and The Drunken Boat*

Guillermo Rosales, The Halfway House
Evelio Rosero, The Armies
Fran Ross, Oreo
Joseph Roth, The Emperor's Tomb
   The Hotel Years
Raymond Roussel, Locus Solus
Ihara Saikaku, The Life of an Amorous Woman
Nathalie Sarraute, Tropisms
Jean-Paul Sartre, Nausea
   The Wall
Delmore Schwartz
   In Dreams Begin Responsibilities
Hasan Shah, The Dancing Girl
W. G. Sebald, The Emigrants
   The Rings of Saturn
   Vertigo
Stevie Smith, Best Poems
Gary Snyder, Turtle Island
Muriel Spark, The Driver's Seat
   The Girls of Slender Means
   Memento Mori
Reiner Stach, Is That Kafka?
Antonio Tabucchi, Pereira Maintains
Junichiro Tanizaki, A Cat, a Man & Two Women
Yoko Tawada, The Emissary
   Memoirs of a Polar Bear
Dylan Thomas, A Child's Christmas in Wales
   Collected Poems
Uwe Timm, The Invention of Curried Sausage
Tomas Tranströmer
   The Great Enigma: New Collected Poems
Leonid Tsypkin, Summer in Baden-Baden
Frederic Tuten, The Adventures of Mao
Regina Ullmann, The Country Road
Paul Valéry, Selected Writings
Enrique Vila-Matas, Bartleby & Co.
Elio Vittorini, Conversations in Sicily
Rosmarie Waldrop, Gap Gardening
Robert Walser, The Assistant
   The Tanners
Eliot Weinberger, The Ghosts of Birds
Nathanael West, The Day of the Locust
   Miss Lonelyhearts
Tennessee Williams, Cat on a Hot Tin Roof
   The Glass Menagerie
   A Streetcar Named Desire
William Carlos Williams, Selected Poems
   Spring and All
Louis Zukofsky, "A"

*BILINGUAL EDITION

For a complete listing, request a free catalog from New Directions, 80 8th Avenue, New York, NY 10011 or visit us online at ndbooks.com